1&2 Thessalonians

Prepare for Christ's Return

Sarah K. Howley

Flaming Dove Press

Flaming Dove Press
an imprint of
InspiritEncourage LLC
1520 Belle View Blvd #5081
Alexandria, VA 22307
www.inspiritencourage.com

ISBN 978-1-960793-25-6 (e-book)
ISBN 978-1-960793-24-9 (paperback)
ISBN 978-1-960793-26-3 (large print)

Printed in the United States of America

Library of Congress Control Number: 2025905459

Contents

Welcome

to this study of 1 & 2 Thessalonians

These letters were likely some of the earliest that Paul wrote, dated about 20 years after Jesus' death and resurrection. Paul spent just a short few weeks with the fledgling church in Thessalonica before he was forced to flee the city. Paul had been accused of declaring Jesus to be a king and political challenger of Caesar, which brought about formal charges, so the church helped him escape the area (Acts 17: 6-10).

Based on these letters one can assume that, Paul continued to have contact with the group, despite the trouble that had been caused. He felt it was necessary to stay away from the city as long as the (false) charges stood regarding his activities in Thessalonica and sent Timothy instead.

These two epistles are known for their discussion on main theme, the end-times, which is the main theme of them. However, the letter also contained words of comfort with some additional instruction about living godly lives. We find that Jesus himself spoke extensively of the end times in addition to finding the topic addressed in the Old Testament as well. This study sets out to highlight some of the Old Testament passages as well as the ones in these epistles in order to deepen our understanding of the Word and its instruction for Christians today.

The two epistles to the Thessalonians open with a greeting from Paul, Silas, and Timothy, though scholars generally refer to them as Paul's letters. This exclusion of the other co-authors is not only for ease of reference, and certainly no slight intended to Silas and Timothy, but also because it is not well understood how co-authoring letters worked. Many believe that the secondary authors were merely sending greetings. Others believe that letters were discussed together and then written down, usually by a scribe. Either way that might have been tradition, this study too will refer to them as Paul's letters to Thessalonica.

Each session opens with warm-up introductory questions, goes on to a reading from 1 or 2 Thessalonians and questions related to the passage. Then the study moves to the linked Old Testament passages and questions. Each study session ends with considerations for personal application. Additional tips and suggestions on approaching the study for individuals and groups follow.

Suggestions for Study

This study is designed for individual or small group study and is composed of 9 sessions. It is designed to encourage thought and discussion of the scripture, inspiring individuals and groups seeking God to have conversations about the text. For "You will seek me and find me when you seek me with all your heart," as Jeremiah 29:13 says.

General Guidelines for Individual Study

1. Open each session with prayer. Ask God to speak through his Word.

2. Respond to the introductory questions that focus on the theme of the session and what Jesus says in the main reading.

3. Read the passage more than once. Using different translations can offer expanded viewpoints on the meaning of the original text. This study uses the New International Version (NIV) as the basis of questions and quotes. However, any version may be used to provide insight and assist in revealing meaning.

4. This study is designed to offer a starting point for discovery of what God has to say to you through his Word. Because the study looks at how the Old Testament is reflected in the epistles, there are observation and interpretation questions about the readings in 1 & 2 Thessalonians and then about the linked passage(s) in the Old Testament, as well as comparisons between them. These are followed by application questions for personal and group discussion. Writing your responses will provide clarity and focus your thoughts on the verses.

5. Use a Bible dictionary or other reference books to look up any unfamiliar words, places, or names.

General Guidelines for Group Study

1. Come to sessions prepared. Some groups will choose to read and respond ahead of time then gather and discuss; others will gather to read and discuss together. Before beginning, agree how you would like to proceed so all are prepared.

2. Be an active participant in the group by sharing your thoughts and responses to the questions. Groups often have members who are in different places in their walk with Christ and each perspective should be valued.

3. Listen to each other. Consider the amount of time that is available for all to share and be careful not to dominate the conversation.

4. Be open-minded. As there may be various answers offered in discussion, be open to considering alternate viewpoints and agree to disagree.

5. Maintain confidentiality of the group. For participants to be willing to share and grow, the trust level in the group must be high. Do not share what is shared in the group outside of the group unless permission is given to do so.

6. Expect God to meet you in the study. His Word is living and active (Heb. 4:12) and he is present when we gather in his name (Matt. 18:20).

Introduction

Opening

Before beginning the study, describe your understanding of the day of Jesus' return. How do you feel about it?

Paul was not with the Thessalonians long, before he was forced to leave the city. Who has made an impact on your life in a short amount of time? What would it be like to receive a letter from them after not having heard from them in a long time?

Read Acts 17:1-10 for background information about Paul's relationship with the Thessalonian church.

Session 1: Thanksgiving for Faith, Hope and Love

1 Thessalonians 1:1-10

Opening

When was the last time you wrote a letter or card to someone? How did you address the person?

Describe a time when you experienced joy in the midst of suffering. If you have not experienced this, consider what situations might yield this.

Letters in Paul's time were often filled with words of comfort, thanksgiving or exhortation. The opening of this letter to the Thessalonians reviews what happened while Paul was with them, commending them for their faith and the work that has come from it. The Thessalonians were surrounded by non-believers and yet persevered in faith, hope, and love.

Read 1 Thessalonians 1:1-10.

Reading Questions

What was Paul thankful to God for about the Thessalonians?

What did the Thessalonians receive along with the message of the gospel?

How did they respond to the message?

What reference was made to the second coming of Christ?

How was the Holy Spirit present to the Thessalonians during Paul's time with them?

Old Testament Links

There are several references to the "day of judgement" in the letters to the Thessalonians. The first is here at the end of the first reading. Teachings of the final days were perhaps a portion of the teachings that Paul delivered during his short time with the people of Thessalonica. However, the epistles to the church also indicate that Paul is correcting their thoughts and actions in regard to the topic. The response to end times teachings is often either fear or rejoicing, opposite emotions. From the short reference here, it seems the believers were rejoicing in the day that would come.

The "coming wrath", or day of judgement, is referenced in several places in the Old Testament; let us focus on the writings of Isaiah about that day. Read Isaiah 2:10-21, 13:9-13, and 34:2-4, which would have likely been part of the teachings that Paul gave them while he stayed with the Thessalonians. Paul writes that they "wait for his [the living and true God's] Son from heaven." Given the situation that Paul described of the Thessalonians, what conclusions could be drawn about what they waited expectantly for?

In Isaiah 57:11-21, the prophet also wrote of the wrath of God yet to come. As you read it, jot down what God desired for his people. In the short passage of this session, how did the Thessalonians demonstrate they were ones who took "refuge in me and will inherit the land..."? What hope did this passage offer in teachings of the day of wrath?

Application

How do you view the day of judgement – with joy or trepidation or something else? How does the hope from the verse in Thessalonians and in Isaiah affect that feeling?

Paul is very complementary to the Thessalonians. What group (or individuals) in your life would you say similar things about? What exactly would you say to those people in your life?

Session 2: Ministry and Conduct

1 Thessalonians 2:1-16

Opening

What is the motivation for the work or "day job" that you have?

What are the main responsibilities of a parent toward their child or children?

Paul did not marry and have children, however he took on all believers that he met as his own flock. He taught and behaved as though toward his own family. This meant that he encouraged as well as rebuked. He sacrificed and scraped as well as offered generous reward. The example he set was in more than just his life but also his interactions with others around him and his written teachings.

Read 1 Thessalonians 2:1-16.

Reading Questions

Paul says that they spoke "as one approved by God...". Given the context of this verse, how would God's approval have been obtained?

Paul contrasted "looking for praise" and "asserting authority" with his behavior among the Thessalonians. In what ways did Paul show humility while also encouraging the Thessalonian church?

In what ways did Paul and his companions care for the Thessalonians?

Describe the suffering that the believers experienced.

What did Paul express was his motivation for work, or his day job?

Old Testament Links

Paul mentioned the Holy Spirit twice in the first paragraph, and in today's reading said that the Word was at work in the people. The insight that God has into our lives and hearts is not a new concept in Paul's letter. In the Old Testament and in the Gospels, it is stated that God saw the heart. Consider what rich meaning Paul drew upon when he spoke of testing the heart as you read these passages.

One of the first mentions of the heart is in references to David. When David was anointed by the prophet Samuel, it was because of his heart. Read 1 Samuel 16:1-13 and describe what God understood of a person by looking at the heart.

God tested the heart in other passages of the Old Testament. Read Proverbs 17:3; what can we learn by the analogy of God and the silversmith and the goldsmith? What contrast is offered in Jeremiah 11:20 and 17:10 about God's testing the heart?

How do these Old Testament passages open a deeper understanding into verse 2:4 of 1 Thessalonians?

Application

Paul described himself as a mother, child, and father in this passage. Consider your role in various relationships. In what ways are you also filling multiple roles at the same time? Are these relationships mature and joyful as Paul seemed to describe?

Paul said that he was like a father, "encouraging, comforting, and urging you to live lives worthy of God...," (2:11-12). Given your own circumstances today, what encouraging or comforting word could you imagine Paul offering you? Or what would he urge you to do?

Session 3: Believer's Conduct

1 Thessalonians 2:17–3:13

Opening

In modern times we have many ways to communicate with those who are far from us. What is your preferred method of communication with those who are separated from you by some distance?

We often make plans for our day, our week and even our year. However, they do not all get accomplished. Consider what keeps you from accomplishing your plans.

Paul's writings are full of his everyday frustrations and joys. We learn of his desire to visit the Thessalonians but he wasn't able to himself. His plans and inability to carry them out is very relatable. In the nuances of Paul's story lie many things we can relate to today.

Read 1 Thessalonians 2:17-3:13.

Reading Questions

Describe the comings and goings of Paul explained in this passage.

What kind of crown did Paul say he would "glory in" in the presence of the Lord?

Why was Timothy sent to the Thessalonians?

What was Timothy's report upon returning to Paul?

What was Paul's blessing over the Thessalonians in this passage?

Old Testament Links

Paul again closed this reading with a reference to the day of judgement. The letter continually referred to the coming day of the Lord, but Paul accompanied references to the Old Testament with words of hope.

1 Thessalonians 3:13 referenced Zechariah 14:5. Read Zechariah 14:1-9. How did Paul offer this Old Testament passage a different perspective in the words to the Thessalonian church?

Scholars believe Paul may have referenced Jeremiah 30:7 in his teachings about trouble for the Jewish people. How did verses 3:3-4 also reassure the Thessalonians?

Application

Paul prays that the love of the Thessalonians for one another "increase and overflow". Describe what this is or would be like for your small group, your family, or your church.

Paul was unable to go to the Thessalonians himself and had to delegate the visit. On a scale of 1 to 5, how good are you at delegating? Despite Paul not wanting to delegate, he invited Timothy to serve the church by visiting. In what ways could you encourage others to serve God? What things could you delegate to others so they can serve God?

Session 4: Living Holy

1 Thessalonians 4:1-12

Opening

The title of this session is "Living Holy." How do you define holy? How is it we call both people and a night (Christmas) holy?

One weakness that is occasionally mentioned about people is that they are "people pleasers." Why would this be considered a weakness? Why would pleasing God not be a weakness?

Living holy is not unattainable. If a night can be "holy", then the way we live out lives can also be "holy." *Holy* is to be set apart, or different. Paul called on the Thessalonians to be like Jesus rather than continue as they had been living. The contrast of living like Jesus can be radical for some and less so for others. Still today we are called to live holy, like Jesus did.

Read 1 Thessalonians 4:1-12.

Reading Questions

How did Paul say that the Thessalonians were living at the time of his letter?

Given the lengthy instructions on the topic, what was Paul most interested in seeing the Thessalonians do better?

Paul connects rejecting God to the Holy Spirit. What is the importance of this connection in the passage?

Paul urged the Thessalonians to live a quiet life. The term in the original Greek is used to describe inner peace which is reflected externally[1]. How would you describe a "quiet life" today.

What suggestions did Paul make on how to "win the respect of outsiders"?

Old Testament Links

At the time that Paul wrote to the Thessalonian church, many had been pagans before converting to Christianity. They were surrounded by a sexual ethic that was more promiscuous and permissive than the traditional Jewish one. Paul urged the church to set themselves apart from the local customs, specifically through their behavior and "controlling their bodies". These teachings came from the Old Testament as part of how Jews honored God with their whole lives.

Leviticus 20:6-24 outline specific laws regarding holiness. What differences and similarities do you note between the passage in Leviticus and today's passage in the New Testament?

Application

Paul urged the church to live holy and honorable, not like the pagans. What behaviors would be included in the list of changes that Paul would urge if he wrote the church today?

Consider your own life and how "quiet" a life it may be, as described by traditional Greek understanding of the word. How does your level of inner peace reflect in your external life?

.

---

1. https://biblehub.com/greek/2270.htm

Session 5: Encouragement about Christ's Return

1 Thessalonians 4:13–5:11

Opening

When you are stressed about something, where do you find encouragement?

As children, we were perhaps accustomed to a bell ringing to begin instruction at school. How does your church or small group direct attention to the start of the gathering?

The Thessalonians were apparently struggling with understanding death as Christians. Paul offered words of reassurance about the end times and also the difference between the ways of pagans and the ways of Christians. Specifically, he reached for hope, love and faith to encourage them. Putting these on was a reminder of salvation.

Read 1 Thessalonians 4:13-5:11.

Reading Questions

More specifically than death, what can be known about what the Thessalonians were struggling with?

How did Paul reassure the Thessalonians regarding death (4:13-18)? What should they say to one another in encouragement, according to Paul?

It is curious that Paul speaks of honoring God in living while also referencing death just after. How does the focus on life and death assist in emphasizing his point?

How could the Thessalonians prepare for the coming day of judgment, according to Paul?

What reasoning did Paul give for Jesus' death?

Old Testament Links

The trumpet, or shofar, was included in part of the instructions given to Moses for calling the community together. It was used regularly and also in extraordinary ways. It was seemingly an ordinary tool as well as one for special occasion. Paul described the end times were also a reason to use the shofar (4:16), as designated in the Old Testament.

Numbers 10:1-10 described the use of the trumpet. What are those uses and how are they symbolic in regard to the Day of Judgement described by Paul?

Paul referred to the imagery of Jesus' return on the clouds in this chapter, found in Daniel 7:13-14. Together with Isaiah

27:12-13, a picture can be formed of the call to God's people. How would the image created by these passages "encourage one another," as Paul put it?

Application

Paul stated that we were not appointed to suffer wrath, "but to receive salvation through Jesus Christ our Lord," in 1 Thessalonians 5:9. Consider the first time you understood the ramifications of this statement. Share or write out how you felt.

Think back to the first time a beloved friend or family member passed away. Often death makes people ponder the futility or shortness of life. Paul addressed concerns about death that the church members had. What concerns have you had regarding death? Has Paul answered them or are there some open questions?

Session 6: Daily Living

1 Thessalonians 5:12-28

Opening

When someone is departing for a long time, or you are not sure when you will see that person again how do you say farewell to them?

If a friend were going on a missionary journey, what would you exhort them to do among the people that they spend time with?

Paul's salutations were full of short words of advice and encouragement, reminding the Thessalonians that they belonged to God and were to live set apart for him. His closing prayer once again called to mind the end times and offered the assurance of salvation.

Read 1 Thessalonians 5:12-28.

Reading Questions

What did Paul say regarding the leaders of the church?

How would you summarize the exhortations that Paul laid out for the Thessalonians in verses 13-15?

How would you describe the attitude behind the encouraged activity in verses 16-18?

How did Paul describe God's interaction with an individual's spirit?

What final encouragement of the end times did Paul impart?

In what ways did Paul describe God in this short passage?

Old Testament Links

Paul focused on the behavior of the people and the activity of God within each person in this final section of the first letter to the Thessalonians. Specifically, he encouraged them to be open to the continual work of God in their lives, particularly through the Spirit. The contrast of the presence of the Spirit in the Old Testament and the New Testament is apparent here. In the Old Testament, the Spirit came at a particular time for a particular purpose upon a particular person. The New Testament was a time when all believers received the Spirit.

Numbers 11:24-25 offered an example of the Spirit's activity in the time of Moses. How does this help in understanding the quenching of the Spirit and prophecy Paul referred to?

How might Deuteronomy 6:5 help better understand the blessing in verse 23?

Application

How aware are you of those who "work hard among you"? How can you ensure that they are acknowledged regularly?

Sanctification "through and through", as Paul described it, is carried out by God. In what ways or areas is he now sanctifying, or making holy and set apart for his purpose, your life?

Session 7: Thanksgiving and Prayer

2 Thessalonians 1:1-12

Opening

What are some recent examples of suffering or persecution you have seen in the news?

What hopeful words would you impart to those who are undergoing persecution or suffering?

Letters in Paul's time frequently opened with commentary on the relationship between the writer(s) and recipient(s). This second letter to the Thessalonian church was no exception. It is clear from the text that Paul remained in contact with the group and continued to care about their development in the Lord. He also expressed his pride in how well they were enduring suffering and persecution.

Read 2 Thessalonians 1:1-12.

Reading Questions

What had the Thessalonian church done that made Paul proud?

In what ways would God act for the Thessalonians who had been suffering?

When could the Thessalonians expect God to act for them?

What two things were the Thessalonians made worthy of?

How were "desire for goodness and your every good deed prompted by faith" brought about?

Old Testament Links

Paul spent much of his correspondence with the Thessalonians clarifying the coming end days. His source material would have been the teachings of Jesus and the short references from the Old Testament. Numbers 11:1-3 is a primary passage that connects wrath and fire; that imagery was then carried through the first testament, particularly in references to the Day of Judgement.

Begin by reading Numbers 11:1-3. Why did this passage come to describe "fiery judgment"?

Psalm 97 and Isaiah 66:14-24 described the coming judgement. How are they similar or different from the message Paul imparted in the opening of this letter?

Application

What "desires for goodness" do you have? For each desire for yourself, consider also a desire for others.

The Lord will come and be glorified according to Paul. However, we should seek to glorify him in our daily, sometimes mundane, life and works. What three things have you done this week that bring him glory?

Session 8: Lawlessness to Come

2 Thessalonians 2:1-17

Opening

Who were the people who have taught you most and helped you become the person you are today? What was the style of teaching they used?

When people tell stories or describe locations and activities, how do follow along best, i.e.: note the turns, imagine the road, etc.?

Paul called upon the message of the Old Testament to affirm the church in Thessalonica while also correcting the lessons they received from other sources. He did not rebuke the church for their misunderstanding, but instead guided them in the word toward truth.

Read 2 Thessalonians 2:1-17.

Reading Questions

What was the apparent main concern of the Thessalonians about the "day of the Lord"?

What will accompany the lawless one in his coming?

How will the "lawless one" be removed?

What teachings were the Thessalonians told to hold to firmly?

What are the two requirements for "firstfruits to be saved," according to Paul?

Old Testament Links

Paul used deliberate reminders of his previous teachings to lift up and reassure the Thessalonian church. The imagery of the Day of Judgement is scattered throughout the Bible and Paul uses only a few references to instill a sense of understanding and calm in the readers.

Daniel 9:20-27 described a vision similar to the picture Paul drew in verses 3-5. Outline the similarities that you find.

Isaiah 11:1-5 explained the imagery of the overthrow of the "lawless one." How might the reminder of this Old Testament passage (2 Thess. 2:8) have encouraged the readers of this letter?

Application

Who are you teaching and forming into the person the Lord intended? If you are mentoring someone, even informally, decide upon the top three things that a mentee needs to learn. This may vary depending on the relationship (at work, at church, etc.). If you are not yet mentoring someone, list the things that would become a priority in that relationship.

Paul said the Thessalonians were called so they "might share in the glory of our Lord Jesus Christ." What might that mean? How does it make you feel to be included in the "glory" of Jesus Christ?

Session 9: Idleness Warning

2 Thessalonians 3:1-18

Opening

Describe a "busybody". If you have had a busybody in your life, tell how they make you feel. Or tell of someone you knew in the past.

What was your first job? Share a few details about the work you did.

Unemployment was high in Thessalonica around the time that the church was established there. Paul was perhaps thinking about the effort of finding work as much as actually working.

Social systems were in place by the Synagogues, handing out food to the needy. It is generally thought that the church did so as well. So, this admonishment was not to the needy so much as to those who were fit to work but were not.

Read 2 Thessalonians 3:1-18.

Reading Questions

What two things did Paul request in prayer?

What did Paul offer up in prayer for the Thessalonian church?

What reasons did Paul give for not being idle, or not working?

What did Paul want the busybodies to do? How were they to be treated?

How is Paul's command in verse 13 related to the warning against idleness?

Old Testament Links

Paul told of the work that he did while establishing the church and living among the Thessalonians. However, Paul was also generous in his praise of those who shared with him and his team. These ideas carried over from the teachings of the Old Testament and were perhaps also shared by Paul while he was with the church.

Proverbs 12:11, 14:23, 18:8-9, and 21:24-26 offer some insight into the traditional Jewish way of thinking about work. Proverbs 11:25, 19:17 and 22:9 offer insight into generosity in Jewish thinking. Summarize the ideas of work and generosity in the Old Testament.

How did these verses compare to the way Paul presented these ideas?

Application

If you have actively sought work while not holding a job, describe how you felt during those times.

Paul's comments may be taken literally, regarding work, but can also be extended to "doing what is good," from verse 13. There are frequently activities that we engage in that are not "good" or productive. From pointless complaints to overdrinking, we may choose to be more busybody than do-gooder. Note one activity that does not actively promote good that you were involved in this week that you would like to be aware of and change.

Conclusion

Every chapter of Paul's letters to the Thessalonians addressed the second coming of Christ. It was clearly a topic that was important. Paul's repetitious letters show his concern for their understanding of the end, but emphasized the correction needed for them to live fulfilling and praise-filled lives at that time.

What key points did you take away from what Paul had to say about the Day of Judgment?

Summarize the kind of preparation for the return of Christ Paul generally suggested to the Thessalonians.

What did you learn about God?

What did you learn about yourself?

Do you believe that Jesus is the Messiah, the Son of God and have you received life in his name? If so, describe the qualities of that life.

If this is the first time that you have answered yes to the call of following Jesus, please reach out to a local church or the author to share of your choice and find support for your new life.

To continue your deep dive into "Seeing the Old Testament in the Epistles", pick up *Hebrews: Elevate Jesus* to continue your study. Find it at your nearest retailer by scanning the QR code today.

Hebrews
Bible
Study

About the Author

Sarah K. Howley is a Bible teacher, passionate about helping believers grow spiritually and take on the character of Christ. She is the founder of InspiritEncourage, an author, speaker, and trained Christian counselor. She has lived in over five countries on four continents and takes her own espresso wherever she goes. Sarah and her husband support initiatives for feeding the hungry and for expanding access to reading.

You can find Sarah on Facebook and Instagram @inspiritencourage. To book Sarah as a speaker at your next event, please contact her through her website. For weekly encouragement and information on her latest releases, sign up for Sarah's newsletter at InspiritEncourage.com.

InspiritEncourage

Also By Sarah K. Howley

Seeing the Old Testament in the Epistles
Ephesians: Experience God's Power
James: Know God's Wisdom
1&2 Thessalonians: Prepare for Christ's Return
Hebrews: Elevate Jesus

Our Trustworthy God: How Much God loves You, Joyfully
Engages with You, and Trusts You

Women of the Old Testament Bible Studies
Hope: A Bible Study of Women in Jesus' Lineage
Faith (coming 2025)
Love (coming 2025)

Alive Again Bible Study on Forgiveness
Alive Again: Find Healing in in Forgiveness
Alive Again Bible Study: Find Healing in Forgiveness
Alive Again Forgiveness Prayer Journal

The Son Reveals the Father
I Am: An 8-Session Study of John

Heart: A 12-Session Study of Luke
Word: An 11-Session Study of Matthew
King: An 8-Session Study of Mark

www.ingramcontent.com/pod-product-compliance
Lightning Source LLC
Chambersburg PA
CBHW071545120626
46550CB00006B/2582